# Slither, Snake!

Shelby Alinsky

NATIONAL
GEOGRAPHIC

Washington, D.C.

eyelash tree viper

Slither, snake!

# A rattlesnake slithers.

# Slither, snake!

western diamondback rattlesnake

Rattle! It shakes its tail.

tail

The sound means "Look out!"

# A king snake slithers.

Arizona mountain king snake

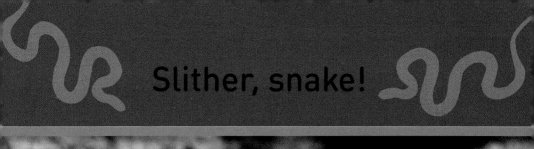

# Slither, snake!

It flicks its tongue.

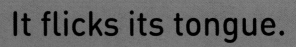

tongue

Its tongue helps it smell.

A cobra slithers.

# Slither, snake!

king cobra

# Hiss! It opens a hood on its head.

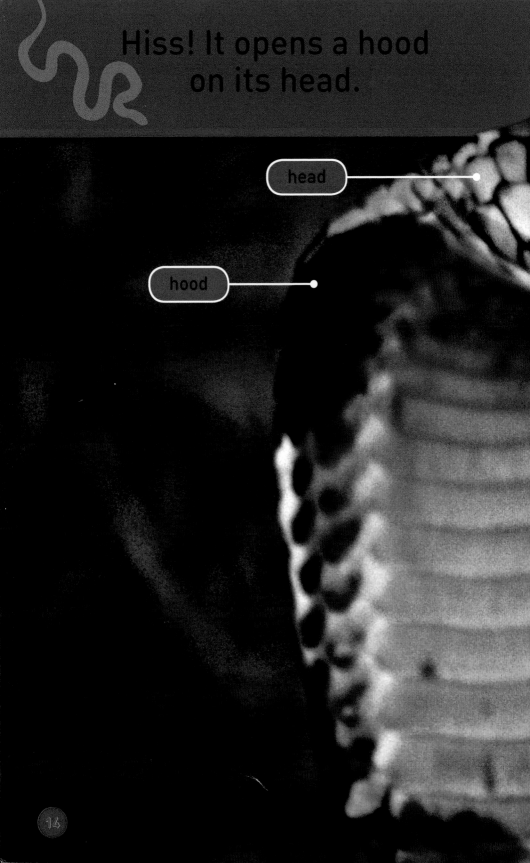

head

hood

This warns animals
to stay away.

A viper slithers.

# Slither, snake!

sedge viper

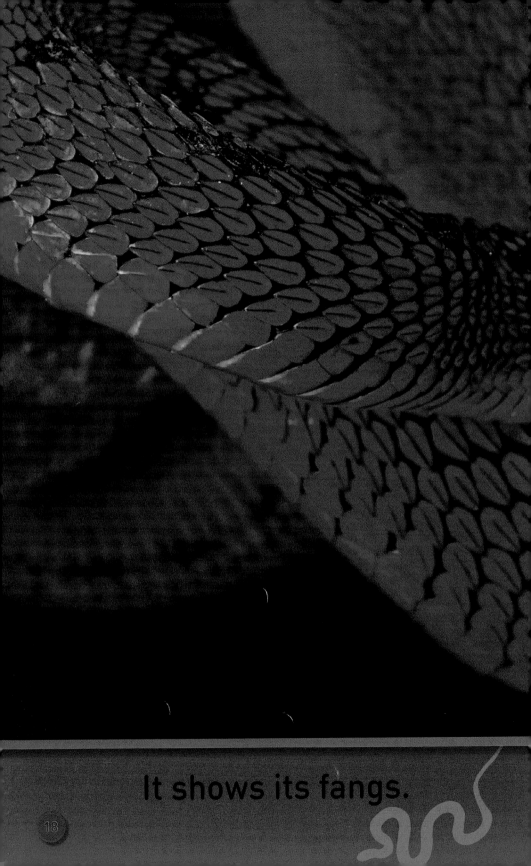

It shows its fangs.

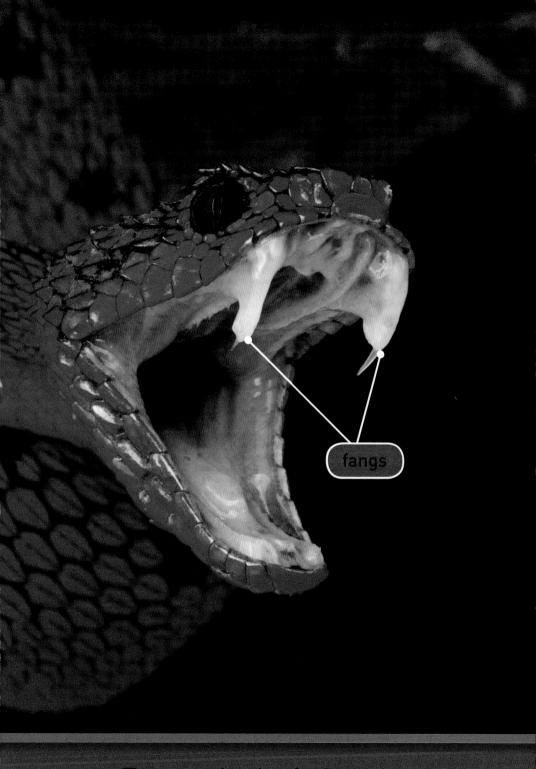

fangs

Fangs help it hunt.

boa constrictor

A boa constrictor slithers.
Its scales help it slither.

scales

Slither, snake!
See you later!

# Snake Habitat Map

Snakes live all over the world. Here's where these snakes live.

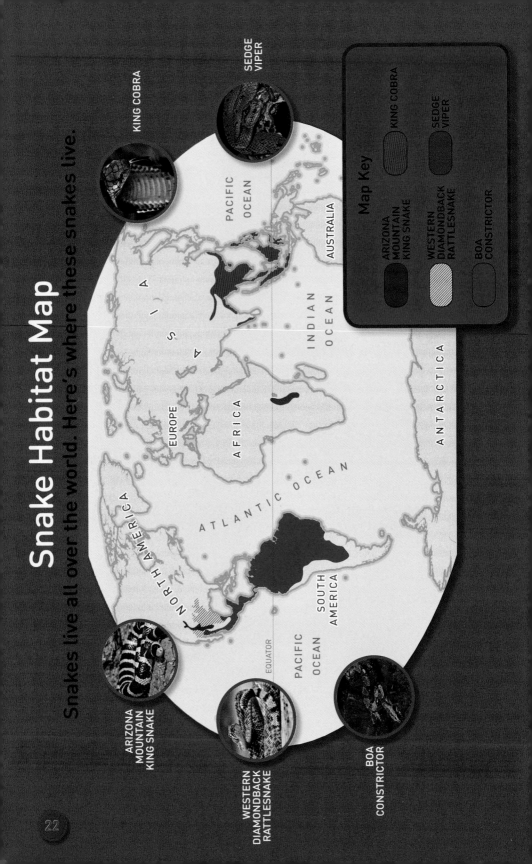

SEDGE VIPER

KING COBRA

ARIZONA MOUNTAIN KING SNAKE

WESTERN DIAMONDBACK RATTLESNAKE

BOA CONSTRICTOR

## Map Key

- KING COBRA
- SEDGE VIPER
- ARIZONA MOUNTAIN KING SNAKE
- WESTERN DIAMONDBACK RATTLESNAKE
- BOA CONSTRICTOR

PACIFIC OCEAN

AUSTRALIA

ASIA

INDIAN OCEAN

EUROPE

AFRICA

ANTARCTICA

ATLANTIC OCEAN

NORTH AMERICA

SOUTH AMERICA

PACIFIC OCEAN

EQUATOR

# YOUR TURN!

## Draw a snake. Label its parts.

**ALL SNAKES HAVE**

a head
a tail
a tongue
scales

**SOME SNAKES HAVE**

a hood
fangs

head     scales

tongue

tail

The publisher gratefully acknowledges the expert content review of this book by Harold Voris, Ph.D., curator emeritus, Field Museum of Natural History, and the expert literacy review by Susan B. Neuman, Ph.D., professor of early childhood and literacy education, New York University.

This British English edition published in 2017 by Collins, an imprint of HarperCollins*Publishers*, The News Building, 1 London Bridge Street, London. SE1 9GF.

Browse the complete Collins catalogue at
www.collins.co.uk

A catalogue record for this publication is available from the British Library.

ISBN: 978-0-00-826656-1
US Edition ISBN: 978-1-4263-1956-3

**Project Editor:** Shelby Alinsky
**Series Editor:** Shira Evans
**Art Director:** Callie Broaddus
**Designer:** David M. Seager
**Photo Editor:** Lori Epstein
**Director of Maps:** Carl Mehler
**Map Research and Production:** Sven M. Dolling
**Editorial Assistant:** Paige Towler
**Design Production Assistant:** Sanjida Rashid
**Managing Editor:** Grace Hill
**Senior Production Editor:** Joan Gossett
**Production Manager:** Lewis R. Bassford

Cover: boomslang;
title page: common tree boa;
page 24: top, eyelash viper;
bottom, boa constrictor

**Photo credits**
Cover, Roger de la Harpe/Gallo Images/Getty Images; 1, Pete Oxford/Minden Pictures; 2–3, Papilio/Alamy; 4–5, Luciano Candisani/Minden Pictures; 6–7, Jasper Doest/Minden Pictures; 8–9, Rick & Nora Bowers/Visuals Unlimited, Inc./Getty Images; 10–11, Robert Harding World Imagery/Alamy; 12–13, Bruce Coleman Inc./Alamy; 14–15, Indiapicture/Alamy; 16–17, Michael Kern/Visuals Unlimited/Corbis; 18–19, reptiles4all/Shutterstock; 20–21, Pete Oxford/Minden Pictures; 21, Pete Oxford/Minden Pictures; 22, Rick & Nora Bowers/Visuals Unlimited, Inc./Getty Images; 22, Rolf Nussbaumer/naturepl.com; 22, Pete Oxford/Minden Pictures; 22, Indiapicture/Alamy; 22, Michael Kern/Visuals Unlimited/Corbis; 23 (colored pencils), Preto Perola/Shutterstock; 23 (drawing), NGS Staff; 23 (crayons), Bogdan Ionescu/Shutterstock; 24 (UP), Danita Delimont/Alamy; 24 (LO), Michael & Patricia Fogden/Minden Pictures

Printed and bound in China by RR Donnelley APS

**MIX**
Paper from responsible sources
FSC
www.fsc.org
**FSC™ C007454**

This book is produced from independently certified FSC™ paper to ensure responsible forest management.

For more information visit: www.harpercollins.co.uk/green